My Furry Brother

Written by Holly Henry
Illustrated by Vera Gachot

2020

ISBN 978-1-64670-823-9 (Paperback)
ISBN 978-1-64670-824-6 (Digital)

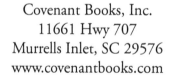

Covenant Books, Inc.
11661 Hwy 707
Murrells Inlet, SC 29576
www.covenantbooks.com

Acknowledgments

To my husband, kids, and Duke—you are the inspiration
for my stories, I love you.
To Aunt E., for your help, kindness, and encouragement.
Ashley P., thank you for supporting my crazy ideas.
The Malinois breed is a special breed indeed, for they are
much more than pets; they are family.—H.H.

To Richard and Sasha.—V.G.

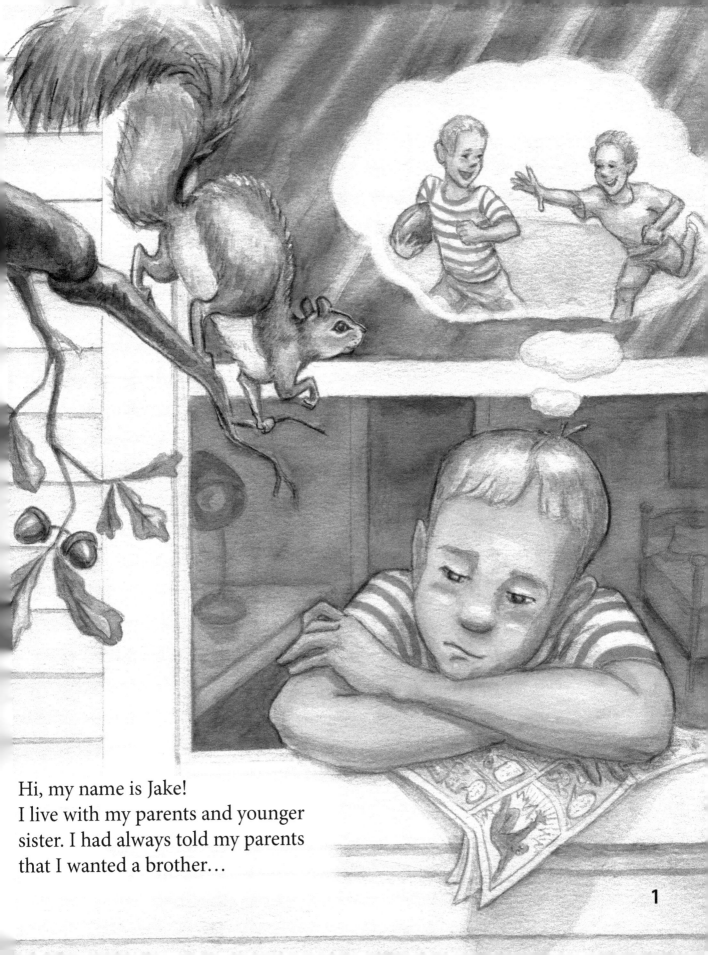

Hi, my name is Jake!
I live with my parents and younger
sister. I had always told my parents
that I wanted a brother…

1

Well, one day my wish came true!

My brother is no ordinary brother. You may wonder why he is not ordinary. Well, he is a four-legged, tail-wagging Belgian Malinois. And I call him my furry brother! We even include his name on Christmas and birthday cards. By the way, *Belgian Malinois* was difficult to say at first, but I finally got the pronunciation down.

We named my furry brother Duke. Duke is the best brother ever. But there are times where I wish he would not steal my toys, socks, or even my food!

We learned early on that he loves socks. The myth that the dryer ate your socks may still be true, but a furry brother is another culprit to consider. He may have a secret hiding place for all these socks, but I have not found it yet.

6

Duke loves to steal socks not because he wants to wear them but because he likes to chew on them. Word of caution: hide your socks when you come to my house. If you do not keep them in a safe place, they will surely disappear.

Besides socks, Duke absolutely loves TORTILLAS! He has even gotten them out of the bag himself when the package was left open on the kitchen counter. Maybe we should have named him Tortilla dog or maybe Tortilla Ninja because you cannot hear him when he is getting them off the counter.

He loves food in general, but that is alright with me because I do too. I often share my meals with him. I mean I like to share, but mostly I share because he keeps looking at me and whines, so I give in and sneak him a piece of food. (Did I say piece? I mean *pieces*.)

So what do you do with a furry brother? You play with him, of course. Every dog—I mean sibling—needs love and attention. Duke's favorite toy is his ball. When you cannot find it, you simply say, "Go find your ball," and his ears stand straight up. Then he is on the move to find that orange ball.

t may take him some time to find his ball, but he can definitely sniff it out.
 am not sure how he uses his nose to sniff out a ball. I mean, does it have a
ertain smell to it that I cannot detect? Do you think a dog's ball has a smell? I
ust shrug my shoulders and throw his ball.

Duke does not play fetch. He tries to be a baseball player. He will hit his ball in midair with his nose and make it go higher. Then he will catch it in his mouth. If you pitch the ball to him, he catches it every time.

Then once you want the ball back to keep playing his version of baseball, he will not let go of it. It seems like he wants to play a new game: tug-of-war. I wish he would make up his mind. I think he really wants to chew on his ball and then watches as I try to take it.

Having a furry brother makes life fun and entertaining. But the best part about having a furry brother are his hugs. No matter what kind of day I have had, his hugs make everything better. He may whack you in the face with his tail, but he loves you nonetheless.

Everyone should have a furry brother because every day brings something new from missing socks to a game of baseball. Don't look at your pets as animals; look at them as family. I see many more adventures with my furry brother. Who knows, I may bring my little sister along on the next adventure.

About the Author

Holly Henry is an author who resides in Southeast Texas with her husband, two children, and of course, their dog Duke. Holly loves reading to her kids, and each night Duke jumps onto the kids' beds to listen to the bedtime stories. He particularly loves books about dogs. She knew that this was a special dog, her third child as she calls him, whose family experiences needed to be shared.

About the Illustrator

After working for several years in the publishing business, Vera Gachot moved from St. Petersburg, Russia, to Texas where she began a new career as an artist and illustrator pursuing her passion for children's book illustration. She enjoys drawing animals and exploring nature with her little daughter and husband.

CPSIA information can be obtained
at www.ICGtesting.com
Printed in the USA
LVHW010401171120
671907LV00002B/61

9 781646 708239